ADULT COLORING BOOK CATS

Amazing Creative Calm For Cat Lovers - Adult Coloring Books For Men Cats

By: SUBHA MALIK

Adult Coloring Book Cats

Amazing Creative Calm For Cat Lovers – Adult Coloring Books For Men Cats

Author: Subha Malik

Printed In The United States Of America

1st printing [July/2017]

ISBN: 1974126765

ISBN-13: 978-1974126767

Adult Coloring Book Cats

Amazing Creative Calm For Cat Lovers – Adult Coloring Books For Men Cats

Introduction:

Suitable for both men and women of all ages, "Adult Coloring Book Cats" is an inspiring and fun THEMED coloring book for Cat lovers. It comes with over 30 classic colorable images of cats to have fun and relieve stress. **Colorable text titles are included as well.**

Inside you will find some simple but amazing cat coloring designs for relaxation, stress relief and anger. As you know adult coloring books are known to have a soothing effect, therefore, this book may help you manage your stress while having fun.

This Adult Coloring Book Cats comes with a decent collection of over 30 beautiful and relaxing cat coloring pages to color and enjoy.

You can relax and reduce your stress with this calming and inspiring collection of excellent cat drawings. Inside you will have amazing designs of cat patterns, making it fun to color and taking you into a state of mindfulness and entertainment.

In this adult coloring book cats, every single drawing is purposefully printed on a single page. So that you can easily cut the coloring piece and make a picture for showcasing and framing purposes.

Grab a cup of your favorite beverage, curl up in your favorite quiet corner, and turn the page to your next exciting coloring subject.

Have Fun!

"If you want to conquer the anxiety of life, live in the moment, live in the breath"
~Amit Ray, Om Chanting & Meditation

DEDICATION

This Book Is Dedicated to All The Cat Lovers and Their Cute Cats. I also dedicate this effort to My Parents, My Beloved Wife and My Two Little Angels!

ACKNOWLEDGMENTS

I would like to express my gratitude to all wonderful people who played a vital role throughout my life like my parents, my teachers, my mentors and my friends. I would not be able to create this Book and many others without their loyal support.

Especially I would like to thank my wife and rest of my family, who supported and encourage me in spite of not giving them enough time.

ABOUT THE AUTHOR

Subha Malik is a blogger, writer and author, he loves to write about self help topics and his aim is to inspire people and help them live better lives.

You can check out his other books here:

amazon.com/author/subhamalik

Visit His Blog: www.storeinspire.com

Lets start
with this
angry
beauty.

Come on

color this

relaxing

lady!

Now it's
time to
color me
babe

Am I cute?

If yes then

color me

friend!

I'm here to make you happy my boy!

Let's Color

This Moody

friend!

Waiting for

you to color

me dude!

Come on

color this

little

beauty.

Now color
this gorgeous
cat
for fun!

Let's color this stylish cat!

Now

color this

alert

baby!

Now Color

This Relaxing

cute cat.

Wanna be friends with you! Color Me now

Another one
for your
coloring
taste,

Let's Color

this

hairy buddy!

Wow this is so cute one, isn't this?

Color this

sleeping

beauty

Now.

Here is

smart one

looking

up.

I am sure

you will

love

this one

I am all

yours

my friend!

Hey do you love this kitten? I am sure you do!

Now color
this stylish
One!

You are

gonna love

this sad

beauty!

I'm sitting underneath a tree, can you color me?

While I'm

relaxing on

your floor,

color me!

Wanna play
hide and seek
with you, are
you ready?

I just love

this one,

do you?

Can you

give me

some terrific

shape?

Am I looking smart to you? Yeah color me!

Looking like
twins,
waiting to be
colored!

I waited
a long to
be colored
by you!

Leave A Review

If you enjoyed this Coloring book, don't forget to leave a review on Amazon! This way others can enjoy this book too!

I'm just a home based author with NO "big marketing company" behind me, so I highly appreciate your reviews, and it only takes a minute to do.

To submit a review:

1. Just go to Amazon and under the BOOKS category, search this book's title:

"Adult Coloring Book Cats*:* Adult Coloring Book Cats: Amazing Creative Calm For Cat Lovers – Adult Coloring Books For Men Cats"

to get to the product detail page for this book on Amazon.

2. Click **Write a customer review** in the Customer Reviews section.

3. Click **Submit**.

Thank you in advance for submitting!